Contents

Of Marmalade, Marbles, & Melodies

A New Litany for Our Lady

Bernadette McCarver Snyder

For Peter's sake
9/25/18 SCF
ALBANY, NY 12208

Liguori
LIGUORI, MISSOURI

I dedicate this book to Sister Mary Terese Donze, A.S.C., a fellow writer and very special lunchtime friend, who has been an inspiration for my writing and my life.

And to Redemptorist Father Norman Muckerman, a publishing pro who was always a booster and gave me guidance when I first became a columnist and author.

And to Father Christopher Farrell, another Redemptorist and an expert editor, good priest, good friend, good Irish joke-teller, and another merry fan of Mary.

Imprimi Potest: Richard Thibodeau, C.Ss.R., Provincial Denver Province, The Redemptorists

Published by Liguori Publications, Liguori, Missouri
www.liguori.org
www.catholicbooksonline.com

ISBN 0-7648-1109-6
Library of Congress Control Number: 2003111288
Copyright 2003 by Bernadette McCarver Snyder

Printed in the United States of America
07 06 05 04 03   5 4 3 2 1
First edition

Introduction

Who was Mary? What did she talk about, think about? What kind of friends did she have? What did she do for fun?

Who *Is* Mary? How does she fit in today's hurry-scurry world?

And who is Mary to you?

Is she only a marble statue on a pedestal? Is she sweet yet challenging like the tart-sweet of marmalade? Is she a melody that sometimes starts running through your head and no matter how hard you try to avoid it, keeps coming back and won't go away?

The Mary of yesterday is a lovely litany— Our Lady of patience, purity, piety—Mother of Christ, of divine grace, of good counsel—Queen of angels, of apostles, of all saints. But might Mary also be Our Lady of lost car keys, dirty dishes, alternatives, yearnings, technology—a new litany for today?

I honor and cherish the Mary of yesterday's litany, but today I think of her in a newer light and with a new perspective. Today's Mary is the brave, courageous woman who encourages me when I wilt, the comfortable friend who listens to me when I whine, and the loving mother who still likes me on the days I don't like myself.

With great reverence, I offer this lighthearted look at the Mary of today, a woman who understands the bittersweetness of life—Our Lady of Marmalade, Marbles, Melodies, Memories, and Miracles.

Our Lady of Marmalade, pray for us.

*W*hat a marvelous mixture Mary is. She makes me think of marmalade—the tart tang of the orange gentled by a delightful sweetness. Mary was the essence of bittersweet. She knew about the fun of going to a wedding at Cana, but she also knew about the biting boredom of everyday cooking, cleaning, and chores. Maybe she even knew what it's like to be in a jam!

Living with Jesus every day, Mary surely knew an interior sweetness, but she also had to face and cope with the bitter realities of an ordinary life—she was the wife of a poor carpenter in a small village, living among neighbors and friends who could not possibly understand her situation.

Mary, the mother, was able to endure and accept the bitterness of the cross because she knew about the sweetness of redemption.

Whenever the ordinariness of life starts to turn my tongue to tart and my thoughts to bitter, I try to remember Mary—and welcome the marmalade of life.

Our Lady of Beginnings, pray for us.

In my house, Mary stands in the sunshine on my kitchen windowsill. She's wearing an apron with a pocket and holding what is evidently a freshly baked loaf of bread. Her son, standing close by her side with his hands reaching toward her, is obviously begging, "Please, Mommy, do I *have* to wait until supper? Can't I just have one bite now? *Pleeease?*"

Mary also stands on top of my refrigerator. Here she holds a broom, a jug of water, and some keys and looks as though she's ready to do spring cleaning. I try not to look up there too often so I won't have to beg, "Please, Mommy, do I *have* to clean the house now? Can't I just wait a few more days? *Pleeease?*"

In my living room, Mary gets to sit down. This little statue shows Mary with so many treasures. She's holding a flower, and in her lap there's an open book plus her baby and a baby bird. What treasures—baby, bird, book, and flower! That's my favorite statue.

Of course, these statues only hint at Mary—just like the photographs in my family album only hint at the gentle grit of my grandmother, the fun behind my mother's serious pose, and the reason for my grandfather's flowing beard (maybe he thought it made him look more scholarly and dignified!).

A statue, a photograph, a pose, a prayer—hints only, but at least a beginning.

♫

Our Lady of Marbles, pray for us.

Some people seem to think of Mary as a marble statue—cold, aloof, apart from the real world of today, removed from the everyday problems of real people. Others might imagine Mary down on her knees, playing marbles with the kids!

So let us consider marble and marbles. When looked at closely, children's toy marbles are so different from one another, so colorful, so interestingly patterned. When **not** looked at closely, a block of fine white marble may seem colorless, one dimensional, and, yes, cold—just like Mary might seem if we looked at her only from a distance.

But when we examine a piece of cold fine white marble closely, we see that it has shades of coloration, intricate patterns, and amazing nuances. In fact, sculptors say each piece of marble has a unique artwork hiding inside it; the artist just has to chip away the exterior to discover its beautiful secret.

The words of Scripture tell us so little about Mary. It's up to us, the sculptors, to step up closely instead of keeping our distance. It's up to us to chip away the cold exterior and discover the real woman, the beautiful secret, waiting inside. It's up to us to get down on our knees and play a game of marbles!

♪

Our Lady of Yarns, pray for us.

*H*ave you ever seen a kitten doing somersaults and two-yard dashes as he twists and turns, playing and frolicking with a ball of yarn? Have you ever watched an expectant mother lovingly fingering the soft strands of yarn as she knits a tiny sweater for her first baby? Have you ever observed a doting grandfather spinning a yarn of adventure and memories for his favorite grandchild?

The word *yarn* conjures up many delightful, happy pictures—just as Mary does. She has been shown wearing blue robes or jeweled crowns, holding golden roses, sometimes sitting on a cloud or flying through the air or surrounded by angels. She has been given many names and described in endless ways.

Perhaps because of or in spite of all these yarns and names and descriptions, Mary has continued to be a many-splendored yarn that weaves through the lives of us all, knitting us together, pulling us ever closer to her son, tying us to one another as brothers and sisters, sons and daughters.

And the yarn she spins is a warm and wonderful one—comforting, protecting, and loving—as only a mother's can be.

Our Lady of Restitution, pray for us.

*W*hen a window is broken, somebody has to fix it. When a law is broken, somebody has to make restitution. When a promise is broken, somebody has to pay the price.

Mary recovered, recaptured, and made restitution for what Eve had forfeited and lost for all her children. By cooperating with God to bring Jesus to the world, Mary helped to restore hope and open the way to eternal life. She helped fix the window, fulfill the law, restore the promise, and reveal the possibility of a never-ending tomorrow.

Just as Mary opened her arms wide to welcome Jesus, she welcomes me and you too. She has made it possible for us to ask her anything. She allows us to pray this prayer:

Remember, O most gracious Virgin Mary,
that never was it known
that anyone who fled to your protection,
implored your help, or sought your intercession
was left unaided.
Inspired with this confidence,
I fly unto you, O virgin of virgins,
my Mother.
To you I come,
before you I stand, sinful and sorrowful.
O Mother of the Word Incarnate,
despise not my petitions,
but in your mercy, hear and answer me.
Amen.

Our Lady of Melodies, pray for us.

*H*ow much is that doggy in the window?" "When you wish upon a star…" "Onward, Christian soldiers…" How and why do these old tunes suddenly show up in my head and urge me to sing along? And what does that have to do with Mary?

Mary's melody also shows up suddenly and commands my attention. No matter how negligent I am, no matter how often I forget her or push her aside for other interests, Mary's melody lingers on.

I try to remember to say the rosary every day, but I get busy and forget. I manage to put Mary at the bottom of my "to-do" lists. Yet when I was in a terrifying auto accident, the words that instantly came into my head as the car plummeted down an incline were those familiar words, "Hail Mary, full of grace….HELP!"

In the same way, whenever I encounter a pressing problem, whether minor or major, the first words that run through my head have that familiar tune, "Hail Mary, full of grace.... What do I do or say now?"

Although I am not as dutiful a daughter as I should be, what a comfort it is to know that Mary, the forgiving mother, will always be around to sing along with me.

Our Lady of Tickles, pray for us.

One morning as I was almost dozing in the pew, a reading from Timothy got my attention. It was warning against "teachers who tickle your ears with false doctrines" (1 Tim 1:3–11).

Ah, it is not hard to think of all the "teachers" on TV or in many popular movies who so subtly and artistically tickle our ears with false doctrines. It is not hard to think of all the everyday happenings that tempt us to accept the false doctrines that look so good and seem so perfect—and would be so much easier to choose than the true but difficult doctrines we know deep down are not false.

Mary tickles too—and her example is never false. As we look at her life with the little bit of information we have, we see how easy and more convenient it would have been for her to say no instead of yes. We see how much more "practical" or perhaps intelligent it would have been for her to choose an easier life than the difficult one she lived.

Ah, the kind of tickles that lead to giggles are so good, but today's tickles are a very different kind—the kind that should remind us more than ever to turn to Mary's example. So often today we need to ask her to tickle our ears with truth.

Our Lady of Remembrances, pray for us.

The thought of Mary brings forth so many remembrances, but one of the less-important ones stands out. The memory is of the year when my "career" took me to a new job in a new city. I moved there all alone, on my own for the first time. Since I didn't know anyone yet, I had plenty of time to wander about and explore the new city. On my lunch hour, I frequently went window shopping.

In the window of an elegant jewelry store near my office sat an expensive Hummel statue of Mary. For a long time I admired it from afar. Then, after I had earned enough paychecks to open a tiny savings account, I glanced in that window one day and saw they were having a huge sale. Throwing caution and my savings to the wind, I stepped inside and purchased the Hummel.

For years, this was one of my most prized possessions, and I handled it very carefully. Then one day as I was dusting, I was horrified to discover that Mary's halo was chipped. How did this happen? Who could I blame? At first I was angry, and then I began to giggle. How appropriate—something I treasured almost too much now had a chip—and in a halo! I still love the Hummel, and it still sits in an honored place in my living room. But every time I pass it, I notice the chip.

Mary has reminded me again that God treasures me and loves me, even with my imperfections—even with the chips in my halo!

Our Lady of Alternatives, pray for us.

Sometimes life seems to close the door, nail shut the windows, and bar the gate. There's no way out. No hope. No alternative to despair.

Mary understands closed doors and sealed-tight windows. For the whole human race—shut out of the Garden of Eden, knocking on the locked gate to heaven—she brought forth the promise, the alternative to hopelessness.

Mary opened the door, flung wide the windows, and gave us a son who would unlock the gates and welcome us in. Yet Mary's work was not finished. Every time we see her in Scripture—in Bethlehem and Egypt and the Temple, at Cana and Calvary—she shows us an alternative to doubt or fear, to hopelessness or even hesitation.

Mary's actions always seem to echo the words the angel spoke to the shepherds on that first Christmas, "You have nothing to fear! I come to proclaim the good news to you" (Lk 2:8–10).

Today, Mary still proclaims the Good News. The door is open. The gate has been unlocked.

Our Lady of Contrasts, pray for us.

If we gathered together a group of people who had been stuck in a traffic jam, an elevator, or a sneak movie preview and asked each to describe the experience, we'd probably get as many different ideas as there were people. So it is with Mary. People picture her or think of her in as many ways as there are shadings in a sunset.

If you were asked to describe a sunset, how could you do it? If you were asked to describe Mary, what would you say?

Would you say Mary is perfect and unapproachable or warm and loving and always approachable? Would you say Mary was a follower or a leader? Would you describe her as conformist or as the first liberated woman?

However you think of Mary, think of her often. As you get to know her better, you may find new and surprising lessons to be learned from the soft, strong, delicate, daring, many-shaded, amazing Mary.

Our Lady of Yearnings, pray for us.

*H*ankering. Hungering. Wanting. Wishing. Waiting. What pain can come from yearning. You've known it. I've felt it. We've all wished it could go away.

You might have wished for a better job, a newer home, a more secure future. You might have yearned for friendship or good health or a release from worry or stress. You might have hungered for fame and fortune or adventure and excitement.

Mary might have yearned for just the normal life of a young girl, free from commitment and destiny and exclusivity. She might have wished that God had let her be just another girl next door, one of the crowd, safe in her little village, protected by her anonymity. But that was not to be. Mary had been chosen.

You and I—and everyone else—have also been chosen for a special place in God's wide, wonderful world. Yearn, then, to fill that place and answer the call and put aside your yearning for what might have been—just as Mary did.

Our Lady of Helpfulness, pray for us.

*I*t sure helps to have friends in high places! When you need a loan, it doesn't hurt if you just happen to be best friends with the bank president! When the car breaks down or the kitchen sink stops up, it's nice to be on speaking terms with somebody who's handy with tools. And when you need a reference for a job or a *realllly* big favor or maybe an invitation to join a special club, it helps to have an "advocate"—someone who can speak for you, plead your case, get your foot in the door.

Mary is certainly a friend in a high place, and she's never too busy to listen when you ask her to help you with either big favors or little everyday aggravations, such as spilled milk or changed plans. But you can also ask her for the most important favor of all. You can ask her to be your advocate, to plead your case with her Son, and to help you live so that you'll get an invitation to—or at least get a foot in the door of—that special club known as heaven.

Our Lady of Leadership, pray for us.

*M*ary was never asked to be a Scout leader or the nose-counter on a field trip. She never had to report to an office and take charge of the project of the day. She never had to be the chairwoman of a parish fund-raiser or the conductor waving a baton in front of a symphony orchestra. But Mary knew about leadership. She knew how to lead softly and unobtrusively.

At Cana, she did not order or challenge her Son. She did not scream or shout as a mother might today, pressuring her son to perform the miracle of bringing up his grades or cleaning his room.

Mary was a woman expected to stay in the background. Yet she spoke up when she felt it was necessary, as she did at Cana. And she probably used her "influence" on many occasions that are not reported in the Bible.

Mary is still a leader today. When we look to Mary, she will lead us gently and quietly in only one direction—to her Son.

Our Lady of Adjectives, pray for us.

*A*n adjective helps us to better understand or picture something or someone—a thundering waterfall, a turreted castle, a square-jawed actor, a stylish model.

Mothers love adjectives. They can't resist telling people how smart, talented, helpful, or successful their children are.

Like other mothers, Mary is the adjective that always points toward her Son. She shows us his humanity, his reality. Mary shows us Jesus, the infant Messiah; Jesus, the boy teaching in the Temple; Jesus, the man of miracles; Jesus, her beloved son hanging on a cross and lying in a tomb. Finally, she shows us Jesus, the risen, the ascended, the victorious.

Joyful, sorrowful, glorious, luminous—all the mysteries of Mary's rosary describe the events in the life of Jesus. They tell us stories of Mary's wonderful child and the adjectives she uses to describe her little boy grown into glory—her Son, our Savior.

♪

Our Lady of Options, pray for us.

A birth announcement! Good news! Or is it? When a young married couple announces that their first baby is on the way, everyone starts oohing and aahing and buying little pink and blue ruffly things. But when the situation isn't that ideal, news of a baby on the way can trigger worry and maybe even panic.

Mary certainly had reason to worry. She had done no wrong, yet she would be blamed, and her life would be changed forever.

But Mary had an option, a choice. She could have said, "No. No thanks. Send this baby to someone else." Instead, Mary, deeply rooted in faith, knew that this was a role God had chosen just for her. Mary humbly accepted her chosen role, and the Annunciation became the Good News.

Mary's "yes" showed us all that we need to keep digging until we, too, are so deeply rooted in faith that we will be able to say "yes" to the right choices.

Our Lady of Searching, pray for us.

*H*umans are always searching. Some wonder if they'd be happier living in another part of town. Some consider whether they need a different kind of house. Still others start thinking that maybe they should move to a new city. Others read about owning their own business, learning welding, or teaching themselves to be a portrait or a house painter—all in pursuit of a new career. All of these can be ways to grow and lead a more fulfilling life.

Mary never did any of those things, but she can understand them because a lot of people her Son met were searching too.

God must have put a searching gene in humans because we can't resist that pursuit of happiness. Even when we're not actively out there looking, we're thinking about it, mentally searching and wondering. Mary is a guide who can show us that while we're wandering around we should be searching first for her Son—so we can get directions from him!

Our Lady of Tintinnabulation, pray for us.

*W*hen we gently tap a fine crystal glass, it resounds with a clear, bell-like tone. Always. It never disappoints. When we strike a perfectly made church bell, it tolls loudly and clearly, echoing for miles with a pure true sound. Always. Never fails. It was the same with Mary. Her response to God always rang true. Always. Her life never sounded a false note.

What about your life? When others look at you, do your actions ring true? Sometimes young people excuse their actions by saying, "I have to do this. Everybody else is doing it." Have you outgrown that excuse, or are you still using it? Do you sometimes do something that you know doesn't "ring true" just because it's the easy way, the fun way, the most popular way?

Sure, we all sound false notes at times, but Mary's life challenges us to seek a life of resonance, of tintinnabulation, of the joyous sound of a bell ringing true.

Our Lady of Yesterdays,
pray for us.

*Y*es, Mary comes from yesterday. She gives us heritage, ancestors, and memories. But she is also today. And tomorrow.

Like many families who have an album filled with faded photographs of ancestors and snapshots of family gatherings, God's family also has an album—the Bible.

In God's album, Mary provides us with some of its most poignant pictures—a family's frantic flight into a foreign land, the terrifying search for a lost child, the tearful mourning for a man-child cut down in his prime.

Her album contains happy images too—a baby wrapped in swaddling clothes, a father's carpenter shop, a wedding, a son preaching to crowds who greet him with palms and hosannas.

Yes, Mary is yesterday, giving us memories. But Mary is also today, offering us guidance and love. And she is tomorrow, inviting us to a future "family" reunion.

Our Lady of Lost Car Keys, pray for us.

Where did those car keys go? I thought I left them right here. What could have happened to them? It's time to leave now, and I have to have them. I can't keep looking for them any longer. Help!

The next time you're a "loser," think of this old saying: "It isn't the mountain ahead; it's the grain of sand in your shoe." That's what everyday living is all about—that grain of sand that puts a blister on your psyche and destroys your well-planned schedule. It's lost car keys, a lost recipe, a lost sock in the dryer, a lost track of time that leads to a lost appointment or opportunity.

Mary was a homemaker, and she surely knew about those little grains of sand that disrupt days and delay good intentions. She had to mop and clean and cook and maybe even hurry. And in her little village, she surely heard about and knew about the mountains—the sadness of lost friendships, lost dreams, lost children, lost chances. But Mary didn't have to experience two things—lost faith or lost hope. Those were never lost to her. Hope and faith were her everyday companions.

Whether it's the lost car keys or socks or recipes or one of those days when you've just "lost it," you can tell Mary, the mother, about it, and she'll understand. And by her example, she can show you how to survive the grains of sand so that you will not lose faith or hope.

Our Lady of Waiting, pray for us.

*Y*ou know how maddening it can be to wait in line—at a shop, a bank, a supermarket. You've probably felt the frustration of being in a car barely moving through a traffic jam.

You may know what it's like to wait for an adolescent to grow up—or for a grownup to grow up. You may also know how difficult it is to wait for news in a hospital emergency room or wait for a child to come home when it's long after curfew.

Mary knew all about waiting. Can you imagine how she must have felt waiting for the Messiah, thinking of the secret the angel had told her, hugging the joy and swallowing the fear? Can you imagine how she must have felt waiting at the foot of the cross?

Whether the waiting times in your life are trivial or terrible, ask Mary to wait with you. She can help you smile and swallow the irritation or grit your teeth and endure the fear. Mary knows about waiting.

Our Lady of Service, pray for us.

Who wants to be a servant, a slave, a no-body? Who wants to be a maid who sweeps up the scraps? Who wants to be overworked and underpaid in a low-level job?

What future is there in washing dirty dishes and dirty laundry or cleaning up other people's mistakes and messes? What future is there in "taking care of business" when nobody notices, nobody says "Thanks," nobody says "Good job"? You and I are above all that, aren't we?

Fortunately, Mary was not. She knew there could be dignity in honest work. She knew about the nobility of service, the virtue of devotion.

Mary also knew that if we choose to accept a job, no matter how lowly, then we can find joy and satisfaction by turning it into a job well done.

Mary knew it is possible to be of service with-out turning into a slave. That's why she had the confidence and to say, as perhaps we all should, "I am the handmaid of the Lord" (Lk 1:38).

Our Lady of Mosaics, pray for us.

A young woman needs hope, dreams, love, laughter. Perhaps Mary had all that. But she also had a memory—a remembrance of Simeon's words: "This child is destined to be the downfall and the rise of many in Israel, a sign that will be opposed—and you yourself shall be pierced with a sword" (Lk 2:34–35).

This memory must have drifted into her thoughts when she least expected it—when she was sweeping her dusty floor or patching Jesus' robe or cooking the evening meal. It must have given her a jolt every time.

Mary could have let herself dwell on those words. She could have chosen to live with dread and fear, always worrying about what might happen, always waiting for the bad times to start— losing all the todays by fretting about the tomorrows. Instead, she chose to live in faith and trust.

Mary must have savored every moment of Jesus' young life, knowing that the joy would some day give way to sorrow. But she knew, too, that the mosaic of her life was made of dark stones as well as light ones, and both were needed to form the multicolored pattern of salvation.

Mary can show us how to appreciate and treasure the bright beauty of each day's mosaic instead of focusing only on the dark stones.

Our Lady of Yielding, pray for us.

Stop signs tell us exactly what to do. But when we come to a busy street and see a yield sign, that calls for a decision! We have to look both ways, choose whether to slow down or stop, decide when to forge ahead.

Perhaps because of these signs that cause us to hesitate, we may think the word **yield** means to be submissive or compliant or to give someone else the right of way. Actually, the first definition of this word is to give forth, bear fruit, deliver a fine harvest.

Mary combined both definitions. She made the decision to give the right of way to God, yielding to his will. But she also bore fruit, a rich harvest of blessings for the world.

Wouldn't it be great if we could all learn to combine the two meanings—looking both ways before deciding when to forge ahead, living so that life will yield a harvest of good deeds and good example—and when in doubt, giving God the right of way.

Our Lady of Making Waves, pray for us.

*D*id you ever toss a little rock into a big lake and then watch the ripples go out from it, on and on, spreading wider and wider? Just one tiny rock challenging a big, powerful lake—and yet it made a difference. OK, so it didn't make a big wave; but with its ripple, the water stirred, moved—and changed.

Mary was just one person in a whole big world, yet she did something that stirred, moved, and changed the world forever. She showed us all that one person **can** make a difference.

The next time you think you can't do anything to change the big, bad world, remember Mary. When you see a wrong presented as a right, speak up. When your children or neighbors or coworkers challenge your values and ideals, defend your beliefs.

You, too, can make ripples—and maybe waves. You, too, can make a difference.

Our Lady of Remedies, pray for us.

Great aunt Nelly had a remedy for everything—hot tea and soda crackers. And sometimes that's all you need. But what if you get a snakebite or a brown recluse spider bite—or pneumonia or ptomaine poisoning? Before the poison attacks your system and destroys it, you had better look for a remedy, an antidote, stronger than hot tea!

Throughout the centuries, Mary has been an antidote to counteract the poisons of the world. She's done this by being the symbol of purity, innocence, obedience, and downright goodness.

Today's society has lots of poisons—immorality depicted as the "normal" way of life, constant pressure to be possessed by more and more material goods, false values, and false "gods."

Mary is still the antidote—a role model for all ages, a call to value purity and innocence, obedience and goodness. But in today's busyness you might forget to take the medicine as directed! It's so easy to accept what's being served and swallow the poisons before you realize it. That's why it's important to have regular checkups to look for symptoms, so before it's too late, you can turn to Mary's antidote!

Hot tea, soda crackers, and Mary may be just the dose needed for a happy, healthy future.

Our Lady of Deadlines, pray for us.

Gotta hurry, gotta scurry, gotta get things done. Gotta wrap that gift in time for the birthday party, gotta pay that bill that's due, gotta rush over to help a friend who has a sudden emergency.

Mary probably gave gifts, reminded Joseph to pay bills, and dropped everything to help a friend or neighbor in need. She didn't have to be on time to meet the school bus or hurry to catch a train or plane. But she did have to hurry to pack and leave on a journey with Joseph to pay those taxes and she did have to bundle up her newborn to flee into Egypt. She knew about help and hurry.

Mary didn't have the kind of deadlines that we do today; despite all our labor-saving devices, we always seem to have more things to do and less time in which to do them. Mary didn't have to be on time for meetings and haircut appointments and baseball, football, or soccer games. But she surely did have deadlines in her life.

Maybe Mary can understand the stress of today's modern busy-busy days, but she must question our insistent need to do more. She may wonder why we so seldom take time for quiet prayer and meditation, since that was her soothing balm, her mother's helper, her source of strength and courage to live a life of grace.

When we look at Mary, shouldn't we wonder too? Shouldn't we begin to tap into that same source of strength?

Even if we have to hurry and scurry to meet deadlines, couldn't we treat ourselves by including a daily deadline for a quiet "time-out"—like Mary did?

Our Lady of the Garden, pray for us.

*I*n springtime I drive down the street and rejoice in the season's first blooms, the daffodils that decorate the neighborhood with their cheery yellow buttercup smiles. When summer follows, blossoms of all colors flourish in wanton abandon, beckoning me to notice and be cheered. And I think of Mary. I wonder how she spent her life without those cheery daffodils and summer bouquets!

Maybe I'm wrong but I think of Mary's corner of the world as desert dry and bereft of blooming gardens. I imagine Mary as a tree planted in a barren area, a tree that had to reach out its roots and tap into a nearby stream so it could live and flourish and put forth green leaves. But still I wonder, *Did Mary have a garden?*

Her statues stand in many gardens today, but did she ever stand in her own garden? Did blossoms grace her life, or did she manage to blossom herself without the fragrance and cheery colors of the bouquets we enjoy?

Of course, this is all silly imagining. Who knows what Mary's home really looked like? Who knows whether she would have liked a pitcher filled with lilacs or a basket of daisies on her kitchen table like I do? But imagining is what we have to do to picture Mary, since we don't have a photograph like the picture I have of a great-grandmother I never met. And maybe that's best. This way we can each imagine Mary in our own special way.

And if she didn't have bouquets in her life, I can at least give her roses today—by saying her rosary as I rejoice in the neighborhood daffodils.

Our Lady of What-Ifs, pray for us.

*W*hat if? Coulda, shoulda. If only. A lot of people spend a lot of time looking back instead of forward. When you do that, it's easy to drive into a pothole or walk into a fence. Hindsight will lead you nowhere.

Once Mary said yes, she never looked back. She was so firmly committed that her vocabulary had no couldas or shouldas. Her future, like ours, was unknown to her, but she didn't waste her days wondering about what-ifs. Mary evidently lived in the moment, cherishing each precious day God gave her.

Have you noticed that when you waste time looking back, it can drive you into a pothole of anger or despair or just make you mad at the world in general? Have your coulda-shouldas ever made you walk into a fence that kept you from being able to forgive and forget and prevented you from moving on and moving up?

Well, what if… you stop that!

Our Lady of Aloneness, pray for us.

Mary was the most favored, most blessed, woman in all the world, in all of history—and yet she lived much of her life alone. When her husband died, she knew how it felt to be a lonely widow. When her son left to begin his work, she knew about that "empty nest" loneliness.

Mary might have begged her son to stay home and take care of his poor, lonely mother. She might have discouraged him from running around with that strange assortment of friends he had. She might have tried to make him feel guilty for leaving her to go off and walk the highways and byways, preaching to people who often made fun of him and didn't appreciate him.

Mary was a mother, and she might have done all those things that mothers sometimes do when they're alone and lonely. But somehow I don't think she did. Why not? Well, no matter how alone Mary was, she was never really alone. She had her prayers, her faith, her God. Just as you and I do.

Our Lady of Measurements, pray for us.

Come on! Measure up! Stand tall! Stretch your imagination and your possibilities! Be like the toddler who stretches a neck, teeters on tiptoes, and tries to grow taller as Mom holds the yardstick to measure how many inches have been added since the last time a measurement was taken.

Do you measure up to Mary's yardstick? It was Mary who changed the way the world measured women. It was Mary who set new standards for family life, for commitment and courage and cooperation. It was Mary who stood tall and challenged all future generations to measure up to perfection—the perfection of obedience and purity of heart and mind.

This isn't an easy challenge. But like the toddler, if you keep standing on tiptoe and stretching while Mary, your mom, holds the yardstick, you can continue to grow toward a more perfect spirituality one inch at a time.

Our Lady of Resistance, pray for us.

*O*ne axiom says the line of least resistance is the easiest. Another cautions: The only thing necessary for evil to succeed is for the good person to do nothing. Mary did not believe in the line of least resistance. She did something.

When Mary was pregnant, she could have stayed home, taking it easy. But her cousin Elizabeth needed help. Mary hurried to Elizabeth's house to be beside her, to help her, to do something.

When Jesus was crucified, Mary could have stayed home, mourning in private. But Jesus needed a mother's love. Mary went to him. She was beside him. In the midst of all the anguish, Jesus knew someone in the crowd loved him.

Mary's life was hard. She persevered. Her life was poor. She made the most of it. And always, she resisted evil.

She asks us to do the same. She asks us to resist, to persevere, to love. She asks us not to choose the easy way but the right way.

Our Lady of Independence, pray for us.

Isn't it wonderful to be independent? Isn't it great to be free, uncommitted, ready to run with the wind and do our own thing? Or is it?

Sure, independence can be a treasure and a joy, but this coin has two sides. Freedom demands personal responsibility. We have to pay our own bills, make our own decisions, choose our own path. We can't blame somebody else. In that way, freedom can actually be limiting!

Mary exemplifies the balance between independence and commitment. She made her own decision, chose her own path, and paid the price. She made the decision to say "yes" to God when it could have led to Joseph's breaking their engagement, could have meant living her life as an unmarried mother. She chose a difficult path which she knew could lead to sorrow and loss. But the price she paid by committing her life to service led her to become a woman who has been honored and recognized through the centuries.

Mary never expected fame or honors or even thanks. She had no idea that her courage and conviction would become an example to the world. She never imagined that some day those of us who sometimes feel trapped in the fast-moving currents of everyday life, yearning to be free, could look to her and learn to accept both sides of the coin of independence.

Our Lady of Recipes, pray for us.

*A*lthough most everything comes prepackaged these days, families don't. It takes a little dab of this, a dash of that, a sprinkling of spice, a splash of love, and our own special secret ingredients to concoct the recipe for a happy family life.

Usually the mother—with the help of the father—does the mixing and measuring to come up with just the right combination of serious talk, silly celebrations, work and study, fun and free time, sharing and caring and praying together. It's hard to find the proper balance, the right recipe, to turn a bunch of people of various ages and interests into a well-functioning family! But it's well worth the effort.

Mary, the Blessed Mother, must have had to work on her recipe too. She also had to worry about home maintenance, chores, too many needs and too little money. Maybe she even had to settle an occasional conflict or crisis. Jesus was divine but also human—a baby, a toddler, a youngster, and a teenager who lived in Mary's house before he went out to save the world.

That's why Mary, the mother, can understand when we go to her to ask for help with all the work and worry, laughter and tears, that we must measure out to stir up a merry Mary family recipe.

Our Lady of Presence, pray for us.

*W*hen you are part of an audience, what are you expected to do? Are you supposed to just sit there and wait for something to happen? No, not really. You have to listen or you'll miss the best jokes, the subtle meanings of the plot, the shadings of the music. You aren't supposed to be just a blob. You're supposed to react to and interact with what you see and hear and feel. You're supposed to be present—alert, aware, responsive.

Mary was a good audience. She listened. When the angel spoke, she was aware of all the message implied, all that God was asking. She was "present" to the awesome miracle of the moment.

Are you a good audience? Are you present to the miracles all around you? Do you listen? Have you heard God's "annunciations" to you as Mary did? Every day, in many ways, God speaks to you too—telling you of his love and protection and asking you to do his work.

Don't just be a blob in the theater of life. Listen, react, respond—and applaud!

Our Lady of Riddles, pray for us.

Children—and adults—have always loved guessing games. That's why crossword puzzles, mystery stories, and riddles have always been so popular. Everyone loves to wonder and work out, speculate and suppose.

Maybe that's why Mary's children always wonder about her. Was she pretty? Was she a good cook? Did she have a "best friend" who visited over the back fence or came over for lunch? Did she have Sunday (or Sabbath) clothes to wear to the Temple, as well as her workaday, everyday clothes? Did she sing or hum as she worked? Did she make birthday cakes for Jesus? Did she laugh at Joseph's jokes?

Yes, we can play a guessing game about Mary. Since Scripture gives us so few details, Mary remains a riddle, an enigma. But that's OK. We like puzzles, mysteries, and riddles. And we like Mary.

Scripture does tell us about Mary's faithfulness, love, and loyalty. And that's all we really need to know to get started. Let the games begin!

Our Lady of Parades, pray for us.

*M*ary knew her place—and it was usually in the background. She didn't call attention to herself or try to take the spotlight away from her son. She didn't march in the parade, but she was there on the sidelines, watching and clapping her hands. And yet, in her own quiet way, she did make herself known as an unparalleled, unforgettable woman.

Although Mary is mentioned in Scripture only a few times, each occasion is a momentous one. We see her with an angel who is announcing the Messiah. Mary is listening. Then, of course, we see her as one of the central characters in the Christmas story. She is kneeling and adoring. We see her in the crowd, watching Jesus carry the cross. She doesn't push forward. She waits until she is noticed and called out. We see her quietly weeping at the foot of the cross. And then we see her, a woman, with the apostles in the upper room. With them, she is waiting—for the coming of the Holy Spirit.

When it really mattered, Mary was always there. She knew her place, and that place was wherever God called her. She wasn't in the background because she was a weak woman. She was there because she was a strong woman, strong enough to be willing to answer the call wherever she was needed. Some of us are called to lead the parade, and some of us are called to serve where we are needed. We are all called to follow Mary's example.

Our Lady of Evergreens, pray for us.

*E*ver green. Ever fresh. Ever fragrant. Like the sturdy pine, fir, and yew, Mary endures.

While other trees lose their leaves and their green freshness changes into bleak bare limbs silhouetted against winter skies, the evergreen trees remain ever green. In the midst of bitter cold, against the wintry winds and bleak blankets of snow, the evergreens stand staunch and true, decorating my lawn and reminding me that the green of spring will come again.

In my life, when there's a drought and all turns brown, when there's a freeze and all turns to ice, I can look to the enduring evergreens. Those pines, firs, cedars, and yews promise me that the world will once again turn green, with new buds bursting forth, flowers blossoming, birds nesting, bleakness turning to beauty.

For me, for you, Mary, like her son, is the evergreen that decorates the landscape of life—a promise of spring after winter, life after death, resurrection.

Our Lady of Youth, pray for us.

*H*ow easy it is to criticize or make jokes about teenagers—those terrible teens, those tedious, trying, teens. Yet Mary was a teen when God chose her above all women!

Society sometimes labels all youth as irresponsible, unreliable, selfish. Mary, the teenager, was responsible, reliable, and unselfish. And many of today's teens are like Mary in that way. They are idealistic and filled with the fire of youth. Sometimes, of course, their enthusiasm—or maybe their insecurity—spills over and they make mistakes. But so do adults.

Teens need understanding balanced with good example. They need just, unbiased criticism and prudent advice—but only when it is tempered with love.

If there's a teen in your life—or in your future—look to Mary for help. Take your worries to Mary, the teenager who was young and idealistic and brave enough to talk to an angel, accept a challenge—and change the world.

Our Lady of Deviations, pray for us.

Did you ever see a man with his hat askew, flopped over one eye? Or the top layer of a cake askew, sliding off the bottom layer? Or a little boy in a Christmas pageant with his angel's halo slipping over an ear, one wing sliding down his back? It got your attention, didn't it? Mary's life was askew, a deviation, a surprise.

Mary talked to an angel, and that was certainly out of the ordinary. She became a virgin mother, and that was contrary to reason. She was just an unknown village girl with no press agent and no publicity campaign, yet she became one of the best-known women in the history of the world—which is inconsistent with the way the world works. Mary's life was askew, a deviation—but it got everyone's attention!

The next time your life seems askew with everything going in the wrong direction, go to Mary. Ask her to help you turn to God and follow where he leads so you can pull up your halo and get your head on straight again!

Our Lady of the Blues, pray for us.

Somewhere, somehow, someone decided that blue would be Mary's color. I wonder why they chose that instead of purple or orange or chartreuse. Well, I guess blue is appropriate because it's the color of the sky and the sea, and it seems serene and lady-like. Of course, artists, who are always creative, have painted Mary in many other colors. But when I see a statue in a yard or church, Mary is usually wearing blue.

Maybe Mary didn't even like blue; maybe it was her favorite color. Who knows? But when I saw Mary in blue at church today, it reminded me that she is also the one to call on when you have the blues or blahs. Mary's statues often show her with arms outstretched, as though she's saying hello or reaching out to give you a hug. And that's just what you need. It's just what you need when your day has hit a blue note.

Of course, you don't have to wait until you're having a blue day to say hello to Mary. Every day's a good day to visit with the lady in blue.

Our Lady of Above and Beyond, pray for us.

Sometimes it's easy to be generous, open-handed, benevolent, even unselfish. It can feel good to surprise someone with an unexpected gift or to donate to the poor. But what about going above and beyond? What about being magnanimous—generous enough to forgive an insult or injury without petty resentment or vindictiveness? Now that's hard.

Mary gave birth in a stable and forgave those who had no room in the inn. Mary fled in fear to a foreign land to save her child and forgave those who wanted to kill him. Mary saw her son cure lepers, raise the dead, and bring the Good News to people who then crucified him. She forgave them too.

In today's world, everyday life offers us many opportunities to forgive, to rise above inefficiency and irritation and insult. Can we be Christian enough to do that without resentment? Can we be as magnanimous as Mary?

Our Lady of Lullabies, pray for us.

*S*itting in a rocking chair, rocking, humming, lullabying. A mother and a baby. A mother and a toddler. A mother and a hungry, lonely, frightened, or crying child. That's the kind of mother we picture Mary being. And not just a mother with a baby or a toddler. A mother with a child of any age who is hungry, lonely, frightened, or crying for comfort.

Sometimes each of us experiences hunger—not for food but for love, understanding, companionship. Sometimes each of us feels lonely or frightened. Sometimes each of wants to cry for help or comfort, even though we often swallow down the tears or cry in secret. That's when Mary can invite us to sit in a rocking chair again, rocking, humming, listening for her lullaby.

Mary won't lull us into complacency, excusing us to wallow in our hunger or fear or loneliness. She may even stir us to action. But however Mary answers our cry, it will be a lullaby of love.

Our Lady of the Doorway, pray for us.

*W*hen you've had lots of emergencies that have sunk you deeply in debt, you long for a way to get out from under, for a door that will open to help you get free. When you're stuck in a job you hate, you yearn for a release, for a door that will allow you to escape, to head in a new direction. Whenever you're trapped in any difficult situation, you hope and pray for a solution, for a door to open.

Mary's world was trapped in the difficult situation of waiting for the Messiah to come. The people of Mary's world were yearning for guidance, a savior, a redeemer, the hope of heaven. Mary, the unexpected answer, opened the door, released the world from its long wait, and sent it in a different direction.

When Mary brought Jesus into the world, Jesus brought the world into a new way of life. He gave people a new law, a release from waiting. Jesus' "good news" offered them an open door to life everlasting.

So why do you still wait, wonder, and wander?

The world is no longer trapped, waiting. The price has been paid. The door is ajar. And Mary is beckoning, always showing you the path that leads to the doorway, to her Son.

♪

Our Lady of Reality, pray for us.

When you see paintings picturing Mary, she is often floating on a cloud, surrounded by stars or angels and wearing lovely flowing robes and gossamer veils. These images are beautiful and inspiring. But when she lived on earth, Mary must have worn something simpler to scrub the floors. She had to walk—not float—to the market, and no sparkling stars surrounded her as she stirred the soup. Mary led a life of reality. And that's why she can understand ours today.

Our reality is certainly different from Mary's. She didn't have TV, electronic gadgets, computers, or cell phones. Her world wasn't filled with trains, planes, automobiles, and spaceships. Because of that, Mary probably feels sorry for us!

Mary sees all the stuff we have to put up with and must wonder how we can manage with all that noise and confusion. She lived in a world filled with dust and donkeys, and she had to walk to the well to get water. But that must seen pretty good to her in comparison to our world. Why? Because she had quiet days to pray and meditate. She had time to visit with God and grow spiritually. She didn't have so many distractions competing for her attention.

Our reality is different from Mary's, but we have to deal with it. And Mary can help us. She can teach us to be grateful for all the opportunities and blessings of today's world. She can tell us not just to cope with our reality but to use it in whatever way God asks. She can invite us to follow her example and take just a few minutes each day to seek a quiet spot away from the noise and confusion and walk to the well with her.

Our Lady of the Journey, pray for us.

Some people like to scurry about and are familiar with all the neighborhoods in their own city. Some like to travel and see all the sights in their own country. And some wander off to all parts of the world. That's what Mary has done. The quiet little girl of Bethlehem and Nazareth has journeyed to France, the Philippines, Poland, Japan, and too many other places to mention. She is known and honored in remote jungles, bustling metropolitan cities, ice-covered mountain villages, and sand-covered tropical islands.

Even if you're a world traveler, you surely have never been to all the places Mary has visited. But every day you set forth on your own journey through life. In your travels you may have to struggle through a jungle of laundry, inch your way through the traffic of rush hour, brave the ice-covered stare of an unhappy friend or relative, or watch the sands of time running much too fast through your hourglass as you try to keep up with the demands of a busy schedule.

Since Mary has done so much traveling, she knows how much fun it can be, but also how much trouble. She knows about arrivals and departures, delays, cancellations, and too much luggage to carry around.

Since Mary has visited so many people in so many places, she has heard lots of scary travel stories and seen lots of happy travel snapshots. So when you tell her the story of your journey, she can understand and either rejoice or sympathize with you. Maybe Mary, the international traveler, can even help you get rid of that overload of luggage you've been carrying around and show you how to travel with just a carry-on packed with faith, hope, laughter, and prayers.

Our Lady of the Hearth, pray for us.

*T*here's no place like home! It's your refuge, your hiding place, your port in the storm, your safety net. It's a place to put your feet up and let your hair down. It's a place to sit around the hearth, even if your house has no hearth. It's the best spot for warm cookies and cold milk.

The Christian home has been called "the domestic Church"—a place for the family to pray together, stay together, work, live, and love together. And, of course, Mary's place was the first truly Christian home because Jesus lived there!

When Jesus went out to preach and teach, he knew he could come back to Mary and find a home-cooked meal and a place to rest his dusty feet. He knew that no matter how the world rejected or reviled him, a mother's love would be waiting—at home—to soothe and comfort him.

You, too, can go to Mary, your mother, when you're out of warm cookies and need a shoulder to cry on and a mother's warm acceptance to make you feel all better.

Our Lady of All Seasons, pray for us.

*A*h! A soft serene blanket of icy winter snow covers the earth and turns bare tree limbs into works of art—as branches clutch bouquets of crystal in their arms and dangle prisms of ice from their tips. Ah! Tiny buds of green suddenly burst forth into a golden glory of forsythia blossoms. Ah! The sunshine of summer warms the earth and the skin, gentles the pace of days, and fills the nights with fragrance. Ah! The surprising colors of autumn offer us a kindly bridge from the lavishness of summer to the austerity of winter. And Mary is present in each season.

She shows us not to fear the bleakness of winter, but instead to look for and to appreciate its beauty, to remember her Son's promise that the new life will follow. Mary is with us in the lazy days of summer when we all need to refresh and renew ourselves, and she is our kindly bridge between the cares of earth and the glory that is her Son.

Mary, a friend for all seasons.

Our Lady of Risk-Taking, pray for us.

*P*lay it safe!" "Don't stick your nose out or somebody might cut it off." "Don't take chances." "Hedge your bets." "Watch your back."

Today's world often cautions us to blend in with the crowd, follow the leader, and never take risks. Mary gives us some different advice.

Mary didn't flaunt her "position" or make demands. She was cautious when it was necessry. But Mary was also a risk-taker.

She risked losing Joseph. She knew he might leave her when he learned she was pregnant. She risked upsetting Jesus. She knew he might be displeased with her when she asked him for a miracle at Cana. She risked the fury of the crowd when she stood at the foot of the cross.

When we look at Mary—a humble, quiet woman who refused to play it safe—how can we do less? Mary challenges us to have the courage of our convictions. She warns that in the ways of the world, it may be safer but not always Christian to play the game of follow the leader.

Our Lady of Marinades, pray for us.

Cooks are always being challenged! And they often meet the challenge by soaking an ordinary food in a marinade—a sweet or spicy dressing. They take meat or vegetables or fruit or whatever they find in the refrigerator and soak it in a store-bought or a homemade sauce. The marinade adds flavor and tenderness and turns the ordinary something into a delightful something.

Sometimes I think of Mary this way. I think that if I say the rosary enough and meditate on all the mysteries and all the incidents that took place in Mary's life and contemplate how she acted and reacted to these events—well, if I do all that, maybe I'll soak up some of the flavor and tenderness of Mary.

So far, this approach hasn't been totally successful, but I'm still hoping that this marinade will work for me. Maybe it could for you too.

Try it! Soak yourself in the delicious marinade of Mary.

Our Lady of the Worldwide Web, pray for us.

*T*he spider moves swiftly back and forth, weaving and embroidering a design of gossamer threads, shaping a net with a plan to capture something in its web. My fingers move back and forth on a keyboard or touch a button, and I, too, begin to weave a web with a plan to capture someone's attention—and communicate with a friend across town or a relative across the country. Both webs are unbelievably intricate, and they both are effective unless a strong wind tears the gossamer one or a thunderstorm shuts off the electricity that powers my wired web.

It's great to have instant messaging and an Internet that can send out questions and answers, messages of business and of love, as if by magic across the world. But this isn't really new. Mary has a worldwide web that is not disrupted by winds, storms, viruses, or bugs. And it's been working well for hundreds of years.

Unlike the spider, I have no idea how the

pattern of my Internet web works, so when there is "delay on the line" or when the power goes off and the screen goes blank, I don't know how to reweave it. But I never have to worry about that with Mary's web. Her age-old technology is always up and running. I can log on at any time of the day or night—even when there's a thunderstorm or the power is out!

Our Lady of Lace, pray for us.

Whether or not you've ever tied a thread or crocheted a stitch, you've probably seen the intricate weaving of a lovely lace tablecloth or bridal veil—a network of threads interwoven, interlaced, or tied into delicate patterns and designs. Such must Mary have been in Jesus' life.

As a child, his days were interwoven with hers. She was the one who saw him take his first step and heard him say his first word. She was the one who held his hand as they went off to market. She mended his clothes and tended his scraped knee and kissed it "to make it better." She shared his laughter and his tears.

Even as Jesus grew into a teenager and then a man, Mary's life was entwined, enmeshed, wound up with his. Surely Mary knew the human Jesus better than any one, so she certainly is the one who can help us to know him better.

As you struggle with days tied in pesky knots instead of graceful crochet, finding more loose threads than lacy cloths, ask Mary to show you how to get untangled and lace up your life.

Our Lady of Tonics, pray for us.

*O*nce upon a time, mothers made their children take a tonic in springtime. These medicinal tonics were usually made from herbs with funny-sounding names, such as sassafras or yarrow. And it was sometimes a yarrowing experience because all kids resist taking medicine. But mothers knew best—and a tonic was supposed to make you hale and hearty, if not wealthy and wise.

Children hate tonics, but they love Mary. And she is good medicine for them! Learning to talk directly to God might be too awesome for some children, even if it would make them hale and hearty. But Mary is a mother, and kids know all about mothers. So they can be comfortable going first to Mary and asking her to ask God to bless them.

Actually, children of all ages, no matter how hesitant they are about prayer, may find it easy to go to Mary and use the words of a familiar song: "Lovely Lady, dressed in blue, teach me how to pray. God was just your little boy, and you know the way."

Our Lady of Straight Talk, pray for us.

She didn't say, "Maybe." She didn't say, "I'll think about it." She didn't say, "I'll let you know next Tuesday." She said, "Yes." Affirmative. Positive. Unconditional. Willing to serve. Open to challenge.

Mary experienced sorrow and could have been tempted to despair. She experienced change and uncertainty and could have grown discouraged. She experienced fear and loss and could have doubted. But she didn't despair or doubt or become discouraged. She continued to say a yes to God, to her place in the plan.

When you face change and uncertainty, sorrow and loss and pain and fear, you may be tempted to despair, to give up, to give in to hopelessness. Don't do it. Turn instead to Mary, a woman who had every reason to get dejected, and say, "No. No more. Enough, enough." She had every reason to respond this way—but she didn't. So she's the one you can ask to teach you the secret of saying yes, yes, so be it, amen.

Our Lady of Confidence, pray for us.

Life can be pretty scary at times.

Our ancestors had just a few people to worry about—their own family and a small circle of friends. Many of our ancestors never traveled beyond their own neighborhood. Most of them never left their own state or even their own city. Very few ever visited other continents. And nobody went to the moon.

Today, even if we stay safe in our own houses, television brings the whole world right in to sit next to us on the sofa and share with us all kinds of woes and worries.

Mary did a little traveling when she was on earth, but she is remembered mostly as a peace-filled homebody. And that makes her our guarantee, our seal of approval, our pledge of confidence.

If a simple, unschooled, stay-at-home housewife could be so free of doubt, so confident, so faithful and faith-filled, then maybe we can be too!

Our Lady of Memories, pray for us.

One rainy afternoon I was thumbing through an old family photo album, smiling at the black-and-white images that captured poses and expressions both sweet and funny. A white-haired lady wearing a little white shawl beamed down at the lost-tooth smile of a barefoot little boy. A man looked smug in his tight plaid slacks and white patent leather shoes, and a soldier stood proud in his World War I uniform. A group of "flappers" posed in their 1920s finery on the boardwalk at Atlantic City, and a tightly corseted lady wearing a strait-laced expression peered out from under a big floppy hat.

Some of the photos in this album have names next to them and some do not, so I'm not sure which ancestor is which. I don't know whether the pictures tell me what these people were really like. But I love to look at them and know that whoever or whatever these people were, they belong to me. They are my family.

In the same way, I look at paintings and

statues of Mary and I know that she belongs to me. She is family.

Children learn to be kind and helpful and studious and loving by watching the adults they know—and it is how those adults act and not how they look that influences children the most. I can only judge the ancestors in my album by how they look, but I can learn from Mary by the way she acts in the Bible accounts. I know I will never be able to be exactly like her, but I can try to imitate her in small ways. How glad I am that she belongs to me. She is family.

Our Lady of Backpacks, pray for us.

Did you know that the highest order of angels, known as Seraphim, have not two but six wings? Each Seraphim has two wings to cover the feet, two wings to use for flying, and two wings to cover the face. Now that's what I call being prepared. I could sure use a Seraphim backpack.

One day I got all dressed up, in a hurry as usual, and put on two nice black shoes—except they were not matching black shoes. Then, to make things more exciting, I grabbed navy blue instead of black hose to go with the mismatched shoes. When I arrived at the dressup affair, feeling so cute, I happened to look down and saw what getting dressed in a hurry had wrought. I tried to keep a low profile and hide my embarrassment under a table, but I sure could have used those Seraphim feet wings.

Lots of days when I'm running behind schedule, I really need a couple of Seraphim flying wings. And don't even ask how many times I do or say something so inexcusable that only Seraphim wings could be big enough to cover my red face.

I'm sure Mary never had days like that, but I'm just as sure that she understands and sympathizes with me when I do. And since she probably knows all those Seraphim by their first names, maybe she'll ask one of them to let me borrow an emergency backpack.

Our Lady of Special Intentions, pray for us.

Often during Mass, people mention special reasons they want to ask for all to join them in prayer. Someone says, "For my friend Sally, who's having surgery today, let us pray to the Lord." And we all answer, "Lord, hear our prayer." Some people are so shy, they mumble who or what they want us to pray for, and even though we don't know what the petition is, we answer anyway. Then there are those who say, sometimes day after day, "For two (or three or four) special intentions, let us pray to the Lord." I always wonder what those special intentions are, but I realize it's none of my business; only God needs to know.

I often have special intentions myself, and sometimes I speak up and mention them so that others can hear. Other times I figure the intentions are just between me and God, so I mumble them silently, knowing God can hear even my unspoken petitions.

Mary probably had some special intentions

too, and I wonder if she came right out and asked Jesus or if she mumbled them as she prayed to the Father. I guess that's none of my business either!

It **is** my business, though, to remember to say thank you for all those special intentions I've asked for—and received!

Our Lady of Letters, pray for us.

*H*ave you ever noticed how the letter M seems to stand there in the middle of the alphabet like a sturdy suspension bridge, linking together the other letters, whether they're coming or going? Have you ever thought about Mary as a bridge, linking our communication with God, whether we're sending or receiving prayer messages?

Have you ever noticed how the first word a baby says usually starts with M for *mama*? And have you ever thought about how the word for mother in many languages begins with the letter M—*madre, mater, maman, muter, ma mere, mama mia?*

Have you ever noticed how the letter M begins so many other words that we associate with Mary—*Madonna, maid, miracle, mediator, modest, mystical?*

Oh, that letter M! M is for the many ways of Mary—a meeting place, a model to follow, a many-splendored mother.

Mmm…mmm…good!

Our Lady of Teaching, pray for us.

*D*o you sometimes think of your favorite teacher—maybe the one who first made you think school could be fun or the one who got you really interested in a subject you thought you hated? Do you remember the teacher of your first Communion class or the one who taught you answers to questions the bishop might ask on confirmation day?

Do you remember how some teachers could always drag in a "secondary" lesson about morals, ethics, proper conduct, and maybe even sacrifice, no matter what subject they happened to be teaching at the time? And what about the teachers who remembered your name even ten years after you had been in their class? Yes, teachers stir up lots of memories.

Of course, your first teachers are your parents. And then there is Mary. When you look at her, she always teaches one of those "secondary" lessons—and when you go to her for help, she always remembers your name.

Our Lady of Mystery, pray for us.

*I*n her own way, Mary was a mystery woman. Only a few clues about her life exist. A bit of Scripture here and there, a few words of recollection, an occasional incident or gathering where she was present.

If one of the evangelists had been a woman, she would surely have described how Mary looked, what she wore and said and did! But in those days, I suppose women weren't considered important enough to be mentioned much.

Mary has changed that for all women. Through the centuries the world has had to admit that Mary was special, significant, and necessary for the Incarnation.

In many ways, Mary was and is mystery. But what little is known of her is enough to make us call her "blessed," "full of grace," "mother of mercy." What a woman!

And the Litany Lingers On...

Our Lady of Lourdes, pray for us.
Our Lady of Knock, pray for us.
Our Lady of Fátima, pray for us.
Our Lady of Mount Carmel, pray for us.
Our Lady of Guadalupe, pray for us.
Our Lady of the Pillar, pray for us.
Our Lady of Czestochowa, pray for us.
Queen of the Rosary, pray for us.
Queen of Apostles, pray for us.
Queen of Peace, pray for us.
Queen of Prophets, pray for us.
Queen of Heaven, pray for us.
Queen of All Saints, pray for us.
Our Lady, Refuge of Sinners, pray for us.
Our Lady, Help of Christians, pray for us.
Our Lady, Comforter of the Sick, pray for us.
Our Lady, Solace of the Troubled,
        pray for us.
Our Lady, Protector of the Afflicted,
        pray for us.
Mother of Perpetual Help, pray for us.
Mother Most Amiable, pray for us.
Mother Most Mild, pray for us.

Mother of Sorrows, pray for us.
Mother of Good Counsel, pray for us.
Mother of Mercy, pray for us.
Our Lady of Wisdom, pray for us.
Our Lady of Serenity, pray for us.
Our Lady of Faithfulness, pray for us.
Our Lady of Compassion, pray for us.
Our Lady of Light, pray for us.
Our Lady of Persistance, pray for us.

Notes From the Author

Dial M for Mary

I'm being followed! Someone is looking over my shoulder, shadowing my footsteps, making note of my pitfalls and pratfalls. No, it isn't Big Brother. It's little Mary. Yes, there is no doubt about it—I am being shadowed by Mary, Mother Mild, Our Lady of Good Counsel, the Blessed Mother!

When I first realized this, it seemed strange to me because I really never had a special devotion to Mary. I confess I found it hard to say the rosary regularly or call on her in time of trouble or pay her any kind of special homage. It would have been easy for me to pretty much forget about Mary most of the time.

But **she** had other ideas.

Maybe it all started when I was born. Shortly before I arrived, my father, the impetuous one, dreamed that he should join the Catholic Church. And he did. He also convinced my mother and sister to join. Then, it just so happened that I was born at a Catholic hospital.

Hanging in my mother's room was a large painting of a saint—Saint Bernadette—and one of the nurse-nuns who cared for her was named Sister Mary Bernadette.

So that's how I got my second name. My mother, the usually kindhearted one, unfortunately decided to share her own first name with me, and I became Zella Bernadette! (It could have been worse. She could have given me her sister's first name—Oskie!)

The only other Catholic my mother knew was a sweet Belgian nun who was stationed at my family's new parish and who had helped my father convince my mother to follow his dream. When my mother took her new baby to the convent to show her off, Mother Mary Rita took me into the Sisters' chapel. There she laid me on the altar while she and my mother prayed that God and his Mother would watch over little Bernadette.

Next came my baptism day. When the priest was told my name would be Zella Bernadette, Mother Mary Rita insisted, "No, no...the baby's name has to be Mary Bernadette." And that's how Zella ended up on the birth certificate but Mary on the baptismal certificate. Ever since I have wondered, *Is my real name Zella or Mary?*

Evidently the Blessed Mother decided it was Mary.

Years later, my mother, who **did** have devotion to Mary, started a rosary group that met every Tuesday for about twenty-five years. But I did not get involved. It was only after my mother died that Mary started her shadowing. I kept thinking, *I should start a new rosary group to take up where my mother's left off*. I did **not** want to do that, but Mary kept nudging me until I grudgingly called a group of parish women who were acquaintances of mine, but not really friends. I said to them, "You would **not** want to come to my house next Tuesday to have coffee and say the rosary, would you?" They all said yes.

They brought preschoolers who played while we prayed, drank punch while we drank coffee, and ground cookies into my carpet. Then I said, "You would **not** want to come to my house **every** Tuesday, would you?" They all said yes.

The rosary group turned into a therapy group as we offered advice and sympathy to one another for all the things prayed for. And we became friends. Then I said, "Would you like to start taking turns going to one another's homes instead of coming to mine every week?" They all said **no**.

Eventually, some of the ladies went back to work or moved away. As the group became smaller, I thought, *Aha! This will soon be the end of the Rosary Circle, and I will be able to sleep late on Tuesday mornings or read magazines and eat chocolates instead of straightening the house and getting the coffee ready by 9 A.M.*

I should have known better. Soon persistent Mary "introduced" me to a lady who would just love to join the group. Then another and another. They, too, brought along preschoolers, and Tuesday mornings were still full of Hail Marys and crumbled cookies and small and large problems shared over prayer and coffee.

When my husband and I started discussing moving to a larger house, I mentioned it to Mary. To my surprise one Tuesday afternoon just after the rosary, I came across the perfect house. It had a large finished room in the basement where the former owner had installed a stained-glass window! Only Mary could have found a house with a basement room big enough for a bigger rosary group—complete with a stained-glass window!

When I needed a job to help pay for the new house, Mary sent me not to an advertising agency (I had worked in one during my former single life) but to the advertising department of a Catholic publishing company—where a picture of Mary hung in every office. And I could still have the rosary each week because I didn't have to work on Tuesdays!

When my old car began wheezing, coughing, and making a spectacle of itself in traffic, I needed a "new" used one to get to work, but I knew I couldn't look for a real "steal" at the place where I did all my other shopping—a garage sale. I decided to speak to my shadow about the problem. After a lot of shopping and praying, I began to think that Mary didn't know any more about used cars than I did. Then one Tuesday, I found just the right car—except it had just the wrong price tag. I spoke to Mary about this, but she said nothing. After looking for a car for so long, I was afraid to let this one go, so I paid the price and worried all the way to the license office. But when the new license plates were handed to me, I knew all was well. The letters on the plate were MRY.

These are just a few of the ways Mary has seemed to get involved with my life. I have tried to reason with myself that they were all just coincidences. But after a lot of years and a lot of coincidences, I have finally decided that Mary not only put her mark on my license plate but also on my life.

I have been the reluctant recipient of friendship and guidance, hesitant always to claim the bounty of Mary's indulgent smiles and good counsel. I have been the independent daughter, insisting, "Please, Mother…I want to do it my way." I've learned that I can't do everything my way, and I'm grateful for such a helpful shadow and such a wise and wonderful friend and protector.

Mary, like her Son, is a persistent pursuer. So watch out! Mary may be shadowing you too. If she is, aren't you the lucky one!